Stop Smoking

Shed Your Smoking Addiction Strategies For Smoking Cessation: A Guide To Conquering Urges And Preventing Setbacks, Even In The Absence Of Willpower

(The Definitive Approach For Achieving Long-term Abstinence From Smoking)

Felton Stephenson

TABLE OF CONTENT

Managing Withdrawal Symptoms: Effective Coping Mechanisms And Strategies 1

The Tension That Exists Within The Smoker .. 14

Importance Of Putting An End To One's Smoking Habit 33

The Statement Of The Problem 58

Comprehensive Manual For Permanent Cessation Of Tobacco Usage 104

Reasons To Stop Smoking 131

Managing Withdrawal Symptoms: Effective Coping Mechanisms And Strategies

Withdrawal symptoms are an inherent element of the smoking cessation journey, as the body acclimates to the lack of nicotine. Presented below are a selection of coping mechanisms and strategies intended to aid in the management of withdrawal symptoms:

Practicing controlled breathing and employing relaxation techniques, such as engaging in yoga or meditation practices, can effectively alleviate stress and anxiety levels, thereby mitigating the exacerbation of withdrawal symptoms.

Physical Activity: Engaging in physical activity can effectively enhance one's mood, alleviate stress, and furthermore, it has the ability to divert attention away from cravings and withdrawal symptoms. Strive to engage in a minimum of 30 minutes of moderate physical activity on a daily basis.

Optimal nutrition and adequate hydration: Consuming a well-balanced diet and maintaining proper hydration levels can contribute to enhanced general well-being and mitigate the intensity of withdrawal symptoms.

Masticating gum or consuming hard confections: Engaging in the act of chewing gum or retaining hard candy in the mouth may assist in mitigating cravings while simultaneously diverting attention from the distressing effects of withdrawal.

Engage in constructive activities and maintain a sense of purpose: Occupying both the physical and mental aspects of one's being can effectively mitigate the concentration on adverse withdrawal effects. Consider exploring a novel hobby or engaging in a fresh activity, or alternatively, occupy yourself with domestic or professional endeavors to occupy your time.

Nicotine replacement therapy: As previously alluded to, the utilization of nicotine replacement therapy can effectively mitigate cravings and alleviate withdrawal symptoms. Consult with your healthcare professional in order to ascertain the most suitable NRT choice for your specific needs.

Support groups: Participation in support groups offers individuals the opportunity to receive encouragement and motivation from peers who are experiencing a similar journey. Numerous communities provide both in-person and virtual support groups for individuals seeking to cease smoking.

Counseling: Professional counseling or psychotherapy can be beneficial in tackling the root emotional or psychological causes that might contribute to the habit of smoking. It can also offer valuable tools and techniques to effectively manage the challenges of withdrawal symptoms.

Please be informed that the effects of withdrawal symptoms are temporary, and they will progressively diminish as the body adapts to living without tobacco. Remaining dedicated to the cessation of smoking and utilizing various coping mechanisms and strategies can effectively alleviate the discomfort caused by withdrawal symptoms and considerably enhance the likelihood of achieving a permanent cessation of smoking.

Ensure an adequate amount of sleep: Obtaining sufficient rest is imperative for maintaining optimal health and has the potential to alleviate stress and enhance emotional well-being. Strive to achieve a minimum of 7-8 hours of sleep per night.

Engage in self-care practices: Nurturing your well-being through personal care can alleviate stress and enhance overall health. This may encompass activities like indulging in a comforting bath, perusing a literary work, or engaging in quality time with cherished individuals.

Exercise caution in identifying and staying clear of potential triggers, encompassing individuals, locations, or circumstances, as they can heighten the probability of experiencing cravings and withdrawal manifestations. Make an effort to refrain from or minimize your exposure to these triggers whenever feasible.

Maintain an optimistic and concentrated mindset: By maintaining an optimistic and concentrated mindset regarding the advantages of abstaining from smoking, one can bolster motivation and mitigate the effects of withdrawal symptoms. Jot down rationales for ceasing tobacco consumption and consult them during instances of craving or unease.

Implement diversion strategies: Employing diversionary tactics, such as engaging in a numerical countdown from 100 or mentally immersing oneself in a soothing visual representation, can effectively redirect attention away from the manifestations of withdrawal.

Examine the option of medication: Certain pharmaceutical treatments, such as bupropion and varenicline, can be employed to mitigate cravings and alleviate withdrawal symptoms. Consult with your healthcare practitioner in order to ascertain the appropriateness of medication for your personal circumstances.

It is imperative to exercise patience and self-compassion as you navigate the arduous task of ceasing your smoking habit. Please bear in mind that it is typical for individuals to encounter withdrawal symptoms and setbacks during their journey towards a smoke-free existence, and it is crucial to persistently strive towards this goal.

By integrating these coping mechanisms and strategies into a smoking cessation plan, one can effectively manage withdrawal symptoms and enhance the likelihood of achieving one's goal of quitting. It should be noted that abstaining from smoking is a process that necessitates dedication, perseverance, and assistance.

Exploring the Scientific Insights into Addiction

The scientific study of addiction is a captivating and intricate subject that provides valuable understanding regarding the intricate interplay among substances, brain physiology, and human actions. When considering smoking, nicotine plays a crucial role in establishing and maintaining the profound dependence that ensnares individuals. This essay delves into the scientific understanding of addiction and examines the precise mechanisms by which nicotine establishes its hold.

The Neurological Pathways and the Systems for Reward

The essence of addiction resides within the brain's reward system, an intricate network of neural circuits that are responsible for generating pleasurable sensations when exposed to specific stimuli. The pathways in question are exploited by nicotine, a potent hallucinogenic compound found in tobacco. When nicotine is introduced into the circulatory system through smoking, it rapidly traverses to the brain, triggering the release of dopamine—a neurotransmitter associated with feelings of pleasure and reward.

The Role of Dopamine

Dopamine is frequently recognized as the neurotransmitter responsible for inducing positive emotions and feelings of well-being. It serves a crucial role in incentivizing behaviors associated with pleasure, thereby fostering the repetition of such activities. The introduction of nicotine leads to an enhancement in the release of dopamine, resulting in a pleasurable feeling akin to euphoria, thereby associating smoking with positive emotional states. This significant positive affirmation further strengthens the connection between nicotine intake and the experience of pleasure, thereby establishing the basis for addiction.

The Paradigm of Desires and Acquisition
The discipline of addiction science is characterized by a pattern of desiring and ingesting substances or behaviors. Over the course of time, as the human brain becomes accustomed to the presence of nicotine, it adapts by reducing the quantity of dopamine receptors. Consequently, this results in a reduction in the susceptibility to dopamine, prompting individuals to increase their consumption in order to achieve the same gratifying effects. This self-perpetuating cycle of increasing consumption reinforces the dependency.

Formation of Associations

In addition to the neurochemical constituents, addiction is further influenced by the establishment of correlations. Smokers frequently establish robust associations between smoking and a plethora of events, emotions, and pursuits. These connections are formed within the neural circuitry of the brain, rendering it difficult to disengage from the habit. To illustrate, an individual may associate the act of smoking with their regular coffee consumption, establishing a robust correlation amidst these two behaviors.

Acknowledging the Influence of Nicotine

Acknowledging the allure of nicotine is imperative for individuals desiring to quit the habit of smoking. The brain's susceptibility to nicotine engenders physical dependence, resulting in the manifestation of withdrawal symptoms upon reduction of nicotine levels. These symptoms, encompassing irritation, anxiety, and intense cravings, serve as powerful indicators of nicotine's hold.

The Path to Freedom

Gaining knowledge about the science behind addiction is an essential stride in emancipating oneself from the grip of nicotine. It highlights the inherent biological factors involved and emphasizes the challenges individuals face when attempting cessation. Nevertheless, armed with knowledge and a comprehensive approach to cessation, individuals can surmount these obstacles.

The field of addiction science offers insight into the intricate interplay between substances and the neurobiology of the human brain. The effect of nicotine on the brain's reward system and the establishment of connections renders the cessation of smoking a formidable endeavor.

Acknowledging the addictive nature of nicotine, comprehending the root factors, and acquiring suitable assistance are fundamental elements in achieving success in the process of cessation. Through unwavering dedication and a comprehensive understanding of the intricacies of addiction, individuals have the potential to assume command over their existence and liberate themselves from the shackles of nicotine addiction.

The Tension That Exists Within The Smoker

In my recollection, an acquaintance of mine from years ago comes to mind. Upon entering the nightclub, we swiftly found ourselves within its walls. It was at this moment that he turned to me and proposed, "Shall we proceed to the bar and indulge in a beverage?" One could discern that his choice of words was deliberate, reflecting his genuine desire for some measure of solace amidst the company of others. He refrained from smoking; otherwise, he would have entered with a cigarette held in his hands. He could have activated it while transitioning from the car to the entrance of the nightclub, a practice I have encountered numerous times with acquaintances and unknown individuals. The individual who smokes experiences a notable challenge in establishing connections with fellow individuals, as they harbor a sense of unease. According to Johann Hari's account, Professor Peter Cohen asserts that a fundamental aspect of human nature lies in the intrinsic desire to establish meaningful relationships and engage with fellow individuals. We all require the feeling of fulfillment that stems from interpersonal connections. If we find ourselves unable to establish communication with others, we will encounter alternative stimuli, such as the whirring sound of a spinning wheel or the piercing needle of a syringe. Hari maintains that the discussion regarding "addictions" should be discontinued, and instead replaced with the term "ties." A heroin addict forms a connection with heroin as they have failed to establish strong attachments to other sources of support, similarly to how a smoker develops a bond with cigarettes.

Hence, on the one hand, the inclination to connect is innate within every individual; conversely, associations render us susceptible. Indeed, the level of inner conflict escalates prior to and during interpersonal interactions, a phenomenon that is applicable universally, independent of smoking habits. In communal settings, during gatherings, on occasions that involve interpersonal interactions, there exists the potential for the emergence of apprehension concerning potential evaluations and exclusion. Subsequently, the cigarette serves as an intermediary. This prosthesis serves as a valuable tool for numerous individuals who smoke, as it enables them to create pauses between consecutive speeches. These interludes allow for the contemplation of appropriate discourse and how best to initiate conversations in unfamiliar settings. This tool is particularly beneficial in situations where one seeks fresh perspectives and aims to alleviate inherent tension. It is not uncommon for individuals to experience a sense of discomfort during lulls in conversation, particularly in the presence of unfamiliar acquaintances. I can also relate to this situation, though I strive to adopt an alternative perspective. During such instances, multiple perspectives exist, indicating the possibility that the other party may also experience fear of judgment and similar sensations as we do. It is an acknowledged truth. Upon reflection, it becomes apparent that this occurrence lacks logical justification, yet it persists as an involuntary mechanism. It may not manifest universally, but rather among select individuals and under specific circumstances, the apprehension of external evaluation resurfaces. However, consider this: do you consistently assess your conversational partner during periods of silence? Most certainly not. What is the rationale behind this occurrence befalling upon you? Why rely on the justification of smoking?

4
Other methods of quitting
B
In the past, genuine solutions for individuals who smoked were not readily available until the introduction of nicotine gum in approximately 2001. Naturally, I had contemplated relinquishing the habit like all others imprudent enough to indulge in smoking. During my twenties, the severity of my cough was immensely

excessive, resembling the resounding noise of a tractor struggling to initiate on a frigid morning. I, along with numerous other individuals, conducted a trial of this gum with high expectations. Regrettably, the texture of the food proved excessively resistant, exhibiting a rotten flavor and demonstrating a lack of efficacy. An unwise expenditure of funds allocated for leisure activities such as smoking and drinking. It scarcely hindered or impeded my advancement in the slightest.

The nicotine patch subsequently arrived, if my memory serves me right. This was comparable to a transdermal patch that administered nicotine into the bloodstream. In principle, this would facilitate smoking cessation for individuals, as they would not be subjected to the symptoms of nicotine withdrawal. This was accompanied by numerous assurances, and akin to the chewing gum, I approached it with immense anticipation. Regrettably, once more, I observed no discernible impact or beneficial outcome whatsoever. In my perspective, this endeavor is merely an expenditure of both time and financial resources. The smoking continued unabated and potentially increasing in intensity. Did I endure a lifelong state of enslavement? I must have wondered.

Several years later, the phenomenon of hypnotism made an extraordinary entrance. I must admit, this piqued my interest. I held an unwavering conviction that this was indeed the case. I will imminently experience liberation. Interestingly, I postponed scheduling the appointment due to feeling overwhelmed by the prospect of abstaining from smoking once more. Smoking constituted an integral aspect of both my existence and personal identity. Could I experience the same enjoyment and lively atmosphere in their absence? A majority of my acquaintances engaged in smoking. I contemplated what the essence of life would encompass. It proved challenging to conceive. Even within the realm of my dreams, I quaffed on the indulgence of tobacco. It bore semblance to the termination of a prolonged companionship—an exploitative, imbalanced association I am aware of, albeit fortified by a shared past. In any case, I ultimately secured the consultation by investing 100 pounds, a substantial sum that could have otherwise been allocated to indulge in smoking and drinking. I engaged in a significant farewell gathering with my comrade Paul Dowling the evening prior. I completely consumed all of my cigarettes, effectively ensuring that none remained in my possession. I was prepared to embark on a new beginning. I entered the room, encountered the gentleman, reclined on the sofa, and following an hour of casual conversation, I was fully prepared. I indeed drifted into sleep, yet it seemed to be an intentional aspect of the situation. I bid farewell and commenced my departure, experiencing a profound sense of jubilation and motivation. The odor of tobacco in the vehicle during my commute back to my residence caused a feeling of illness within me, leading me to lower the window in order to dissipate the discomforting presence. Being reflective, I lamented my years of folly and arrogance. Nevertheless, the ephemeral euphoria quickly dissipated; as the next day dawned, not a single fingernail remained. I persevered for several weeks, however, one evening, while under the influence of alcohol, I succumbed to temptation, resulting in the loss of everything. This event had a significant impact on the individual's emotional and psychological well-being. If the process of hypnotism had proven ineffective, the prospects for my future appeared bleak. I made another attempt at hypnosis a few years later, upon discovering a new noteworthy practitioner in the area. However, the outcome was largely reminiscent of my previous experience.

In approximately 2006, electronic cigarettes emerged in Ireland. It can be surmised that they bore similarities to contemporary vaping practices, albeit in the physical form resembling a traditional cigarette. They offered the semblance of smoking and offered a slight measure of gratification in terms of the smoking encounter, yet they failed to appeal to my personal preferences. I extensively experimented with all the various iterations that were launched during that period, yet none possessed a noteworthy influence. Furthermore, there was ambiguity concerning the contents and comparative safety of these substances, casting doubt on their nature and efficacy compared to conventional cigarette smoking. Furthermore, it appears that this trend is prevailing in the contemporary vaping landscape.

I made multiple attempts at abrupt cessation, and it proved to be an excruciating experience. On the initial day, I would demonstrate resolve and fortitude, yet thereafter, a somber winter would ensue. In what manner do these things exert such a profound influence on us? On occasion, I managed to endure for a few weeks, yet I unfailingly reverted back to the initial starting point. The longest duration I maintained was during a wager made with my close companion, Liamie Knox, wherein I challenged myself to abstain from indulging in said substances for a longer period than he did. There was absolutely no possibility of me experiencing defeat in this particular matter. It was the customary torment, yet witnessing Liamie's relentless struggles, with an impending capitulation imminent, served as sufficient inspiration to persevere. Subsequently, on a Monday morning, I arrived at the workplace and observed the yellowed digits on Liamie's hand as he smoked. It appears highly likely that he had consumed a considerable quantity of cigarettes the previous evening; a rather disagreeable habit indeed. Upon my confrontation, he uttered, "Jimmy, there is something I must disclose to you." I believe you are indeed correct, Liamie! While I may have emerged as the winner in terms of monetary gain, ultimately I experienced a loss in the grand scheme of things, as it did not take me long to find myself accompanying Liamie for a leisurely indulgence in smoking and partaking in a few beverages at the establishment's bar.

Why Quit Smoking?

The decision to quit smoking has the potential to profoundly transform your life. Engaging in smoking invariably brings about detrimental consequences across various aspects of one's life, encompassing overall wellbeing, financial stability, interpersonal connections, and physical well-being. Let us now scrutinize the compelling reasons for why relinquishing smoking is a crucial stride towards attaining an improved and more fulfilling existence.

The primary and overarching benefit of quitting smoking is the improvement in one's health. Every year, a significant number of deaths are directly ascribed to smoking, making it the foremost cause of preventable mortality worldwide. Chronic obstructive pulmonary disease (COPD), cardiovascular disease, and malignancies of the respiratory system are among the several grave health conditions for which it serves as a significant causal factor. Upon ceasing the habit of smoking, the human body promptly commences its rejuvenation process. Within a matter of days, an improvement in lung functionality commences, alongside a reduction in the risk of cardiovascular ailments. Over time, there is a significant reduction in the likelihood of developing diseases associated with smoking. By abstaining from smoking, you have the opportunity to invest in a prolonged, improved quality of life.

An additional compelling reason to cease smoking is the consideration of financial implications. Engaging in smoking as a regular practice incurs considerable expenses that gradually exhaust one's financial reserves. Cigarettes come at a significant cost, and the funds allocated towards them could be put to more fruitful purposes such as savings, investments, or engaging in enjoyable pursuits. Ceasing the habit of tobacco consumption not only reduces your expenses on cigarettes, but it also leads to decreased healthcare expenditures. By abstaining from smoking, you can potentially mitigate the financial burden of expensive medical treatments associated with smoking-induced illnesses.

In addition to the benefits derived from improved well-being and financial circumstances, quitting smoking can positively impact your interpersonal connections and associations. Smoking may impose challenges in fostering harmonious relationships with beloved individuals, acquaintances, and romantic companions who do not partake in smoking. The olfactory presence of tobacco, the requirement to engage in outdoor smoking, and the adverse health consequences associated with exposure to secondhand smoke can induce feelings of tension and unease. Apart from enhancing personal well-being and the well-being of others, abstaining from smoking also fortifies interpersonal connections.

Abandoning the habit of smoking has the potential to enhance one's confidence and self-esteem. Considering the awareness among a substantial number of smokers regarding the associated health hazards, the act of smoking frequently engenders sentiments of culpability and humiliation. You demonstrate fortitude, perseverance, and an unwavering commitment to self-improvement in triumphing over your tobacco dependency. The enhanced self-assurance can potentially bring about positive changes in your life, motivating you to make further improvements and set fresh aspirations.

Furthermore, ceasing the habit of smoking yields a plethora of beneficial impacts on one's physical well-being. Smokers frequently experience diminished endurance, compromised physical performance, and a diminished ability to perceive taste and smell. Upon cessation of the habit, the human body initiates a process of self-restoration, leading to heightened vitality, enhanced physical well-being, and an increased capacity to savor the nuances of taste and aroma in existence. You might feel motivated to adopt a more health-conscious way of living, encompassing consistent physical activity and a nutritionally balanced eating routine.

Ultimately, ceasing the habit of smoking is beneficial not only for personal well-being but also for the environment. The manufacturing and consumption of cigarettes, encompassing activities such as tobacco cultivation that leads to deforestation and the emission of pollutants during the manufacturing process, collectively contribute to the degradation of the environment. Cigarette butts, which are observed to be the most commonly encountered form of litter on a global scale, pose a significant peril to the ecosystem due to the emission of hazardous substances they contain. Ceasing smoking will yield positive outcomes for the environment, as your reduced contribution to environmental issues will be noteworthy.

Importance Of Putting An End To One's Smoking Habit

Cessation of tobacco use carries great significance for both individuals and society at large. The choice to cease smoking can yield wide-ranging benefits across multiple facets of life. The following are compelling rationales underlying the utmost significance of ceasing smoking:

1. Health Advantages: Tobacco consumption is widely recognized as a prominent underlying factor in the occurrence of avoidable illnesses and untimely mortality on a global scale. Through the cessation of smoking, individuals effectively minimize their susceptibility to the onset of critical

ailments such as lung carcinoma, cardiovascular disorders, cerebral infarction, respiratory ailments, and an array of malignant neoplasms. In addition to enhancing pulmonary function, refraining from smoking can heighten immune response and diminish susceptibility to infections.

2. Enhanced Quality of Life: Smoking exerts its influence on various dimensions of an individual's life. Ceasing tobacco use results in an instant enhancement of one's general state of health and overall standard of living. It improves physical conditioning, augments vitality, and boosts the capacity to participate in physical activities without encountering respiratory difficulties. Additionally, the cessation of smoking has the potential to enhance one's mental well-being,

thereby diminishing symptoms of anxiety, depression, and stress.

3. Monetary Savings: Tobacco consumption is a costly vice that can significantly deplete an individual's financial reservoir. Ceasing tobacco use leads to significant financial savings over an extended period, as the funds formerly dedicated to purchasing cigarettes can be redirected towards more rewarding pursuits, such as exploring new destinations, engaging in personal hobbies, or bolstering one's savings for prospective needs.

4. Safeguarding the Well-being of Loved Ones: Smoking inherently endangers both the smoker and presents considerable health hazards to individuals exposed to secondhand smoke. By renouncing the habit of smoking, individuals safeguard the well-being of their dear ones against the

perils of secondhand smoke, thereby diminishing the likelihood of respiratory ailments, cardiovascular disorders, and various other health complications that are interconnected.

5. Ecological Consequences: The act of smoking cigarettes imposes adverse impacts on the environment. Cessation of tobacco consumption positively contributes to the preservation of a pristine and salubrious environment through the mitigation of atmospheric pollutants, prevention of the unsightly presence of discarded cigarette remnants, and a reduction in the ecological repercussions associated with tobacco cultivation, encompassing deforestation and the intensive use of chemicals.

6. Exemplary Figure for Others: Abstaining from smoking can serve as a source of inspiration and exert a

beneficial influence on those around us. Through embodying admirable behavior and exhibiting the capability to triumph over addiction, individuals who cease smoking possess the power to inspire those around them, including their loved ones and even acquaintances, to embark on a path towards enhanced well-being.

In summary, the act of ceasing tobacco consumption is crucial in the context of individual well-being, physical health, and societal benefit. By opting to cease the habit of smoking, individuals not only enhance the quality of their own lives but also generate a positive influence on the well-being of those in their vicinity, ultimately contributing to a healthier, more pristine, and sustainable future.

Enhancing Resilience through Meditation and Mindfulness Techniques

In the process of undertaking the endeavor to cease smoking, the utilization of meditation and mindfulness practices can prove to be highly advantageous mechanisms for cultivating endurance and effectively mitigating urges. These activities foster a sense of self-awareness, facilitate staying fully engaged in the present, and enable individuals to effectively address obstacles with utmost lucidity and composure. Incorporating the practice of meditation and mindfulness into your daily regimen will establish a robust basis for effectively managing the challenges and fluctuations associated with the cessation of smoking.

Understanding Meditation and Mindfulness:

Meditation: Meditation entails the deliberate and disciplined act of directing one's attention to a particular object or focal point, with the aim of efficiently disengaging from the incessant flow of chaotic and disorganized thoughts that may be inundating the mind. It fosters cognitive lucidity, serenity, and an inherent tranquility.

Mindfulness: Mindfulness entails the deliberate cultivation of an unwavering state of complete presence and attentiveness, in which one consciously observes their thoughts, emotions, and sensory experiences without any kind of evaluative discernment. It fosters the cultivation of tolerance and nurtures a sense of kindness towards oneself.

Effective Strategies for Engaging in Meditation and Cultivating Mindfulness:

1. Breath-Focused Meditation: Locate a tranquil setting and direct your attentiveness towards your breathing. Take a deep breath, gradually counting

up to four, and then exhale in a slow manner. In the event that your mind begins to drift, kindly redirect your attention back towards your breathing.

2. Guided Body Scan Meditation: Assume a comfortable reclining position and direct your focus towards each individual region of your body, commencing from your feet and gradually progressing towards your head. Observe any sensations or feelings of tension and release them as you exhale.

3. Utilize guided meditation resources such as recordings or applications to facilitate your meditation sessions. These elements offer a framework and direction, particularly for individuals who are unacquainted with the practice of meditation.

4. Practicing Conscious Eating: Direct focused attention towards the process of

consuming food. Please observe and take note of the various textures, flavors, and sensations that arise during the process of chewing. Consume your food at a leisurely pace, taking time to appreciate the flavors with every mouthful.

5. Practicing Mindful Walking: Engage in a purposeful stroll by directing your conscious awareness towards the physical sensations within your body as well as the surrounding environment. Direct your attention to your breathing, the sensate experience of your feet making contact with the ground, and the auditory stimuli you perceive.

6. Mindful Interruption: Incorporate brief moments of mindfulness into your daily routine. Take a momentary break and attentively focus on your breath, emotions, and thoughts before proceeding with your tasks.

The Advantages of Practicing Meditation and Cultivating Mindfulness:

1. Stress Alleviation: Engaging in meditation and mindfulness exercises effectively triggers the relaxation response, thereby mitigating the impact of stress and anxiety.

2. Emotion Management: These techniques facilitate the observation of emotions in a controlled manner, without succumbing to impulsive reactions. Subsequently, you will be able to adeptly address and overcome challenges.

3. Heightened Concentration: Consistent practice refines your capacity to remain fully engaged, enhancing focus and cognitive proficiency.

4. Diminished Cravings: Mindfulness fosters heightened consciousness of cravings without succumbing to impulsive reactions. This provides you

with the capability to engage in a thoughtful response instead of an impulsive reaction.

5. Enhancing Resilience: Through the cultivation of mindfulness, individuals acquire the ability to confront cravings, triggers, and stressors with a sense of equanimity.

Consistency and Patience:

The mastery of meditation and mindfulness can be honed through diligent training. Commence with brief sessions and progressively extend their duration. Exercise patience with yourself as you acquire the skill of calming your mind and embracing the current moment.

A Foundation for Resilience:

Meditative and mindful practices provide a solid groundwork for fostering resilience as you embark on your journey to quit. As you partake in these methodologies, you are nurturing an extensive comprehension of your internal realm, cultivating mechanisms for dealing with challenges, and fostering a profound disposition of self-empathy. Through the incorporation of meditation and mindfulness practices, you are nurturing the fortitude and lucidity required to surmount obstacles and embrace the transition into a more salubrious state devoid of smoking habits.

9: The Procedure, The Approach

The strategy involves refraining from smoking a single cigarette at a specific moment every three days. It does not involve the gradual cessation of smoking one cigarette at a time. Please carefully review the text once more. The intention is to cease the act of smoking a particular cigarette during that specific time frame, with a frequency of every three days.

To effectively employ this method, I kindly request that you begin by measuring the duration of your cigarette consumption. Specifically, if you currently partake in the habit of smoking 10 or 20 cigarettes per day (in the case of moderate smokers), I urge you to ascertain the precise timing of each individual cigarette. This phenomenon is referred to as coordinating the act of smoking with a specific time or event.

As an illustration, assuming a consumption rate of 10 cigarettes per day, at what specific time of day do you engage in the act of smoking your initial cigarette? Should you happen to light your initial cigarette immediately upon waking, the precise moment you do so becomes synonymous with your awakening time, which can vary between 5 am, 6 am, 7 am, or 8 am. It varies among individuals.

Following the initial instance of smoking a cigarette, at what juncture do you engage in the consumption of your subsequent cigarette? As an illustration, if an individual were to consume their first cigarette at 7 am, and proceed to have breakfast at 8 am, adhering to the habit of smoking a cigarette subsequent to the meal, it can be deduced that 8 am corresponds to the specific time at which they consume their second cigarette.

At what hour do you engage in the act of smoking your third cigarette following the consumption of your second cigarette? Suppose you are an individual employed in an office setting, and you engage in the act of smoking either prior to commencing work or immediately upon arriving at your workplace at 10 am. In this scenario, 10 am would represent the period during which you consume your third cigarette.

Let us assume that during the interlude of your work schedule, precisely at 11.30 am, you engage in a tea break while concurrently indulging in the act of smoking. Consequently, it can be deduced that 11.30 am marks the occasion of your fourth cigarette.

Subsequently, may I inquire as to the timing at which you engage in smoking your fifth cigarette? Is it perhaps after midday, specifically at 1 o'clock in the afternoon, subsequent to the consumption of your midday meal?" In that case, 1 pm marks the time at which you will have your fifth cigarette.

Following that, at what point in time do you engage in the consumption of your sixth cigarette? Perhaps around 3 o'clock, while you are enjoying a cup of coffee or tea? Subsequently, 3 pm corresponds to the hour at which you typically engage in the consumption of your sixth cigarette.

May I inquire about the timing of the subsequent cigarette? Perhaps at the conclusion of one hour, specifically at 4 pm? At 4 pm, the momentous occasion of your 7th cigarette shall commence.

Suppose that you possess a routine of engaging in cigarette consumption after the exhaustive duration of your office employment, during your homeward journey, or upon arrival at home at approximately 5:30 pm. Consequently, the moment marking the consumption of your eighth cigarette correlates with this same hour of 5:30 pm.

Upon arriving at your place of residence, should you choose to partake in another smoking session at 6:30 pm, it follows that the 6:30 pm mark also denotes the time of your ninth cigarette.

Should you choose to consume your final cigarette prior to dinner or subsequent to dinner, at precisely 8:30 PM, it follows that the temporal placement of your tenth cigarette will be at 8:30 PM.

We have effectively measured the duration of all 10 of your cigarettes.

Here is the schedule for your designated cigarette breaks.

Cigarette 1: 7 am
Cigarette 2: 8 am
Cigarette 3: 10 am
Cigarette 4: 11.30 am
Cigarette 5: 1 pm
Cigarette 6: 3 pm
Cigarette 7: 4 pm
Cigarette 8: 5.30 pm
Cigarette 9: 6.30 pm
Cigarette 10: 8.30 pm

Note 1. In this instance, an illustration has been employed involving an individual who works in an office, enabling the determination of the duration allocated to each cigarette. If one does not follow a traditional office schedule, such as being a business owner, entrepreneur, homemaker, or occupying a role that does not conform to the typical 9-5 job category, it is completely acceptable. In such cases, it is advised to conscientiously monitor one's smoking habits throughout the day and establish a personalized schedule, even if it is only an approximate one.

Note 2. Furthermore, it is unnecessary for the time interval between two cigarettes to be consistent, such as adhering strictly to a one-hour or 45-minute gap between each occurrence. It has the potential to fluctuate, but there are no concerns. You unwittingly adhere to a schedule upon your arrival.

Note 3. For individuals who hold the belief that they do not adhere to any specific schedule for smoking, but rather indulge whenever they feel the urge, it is important to meticulously examine one's smoking habits. Each of us possesses a pattern of smoking, whether or not we are conscious of it, and this exercise aims to make us aware of our individual patterns.

Regardless of your identity or current activities, I humbly request that you self-reflect and document the precise moments at which you engage in cigarette consumption. So, this can be referred to as the act of timing the cigarette.

Furthermore, in the process of timing the cigarettes, it is also possible to establish a timeframe based on a specific event. For instance, in my personal experience, immediately upon waking up, I would engage in the act of smoking, establishing a mental association between cigarettes and the event of 'defecation'. Furthermore, upon completion of my breakfast or lunch, I typically engaged in smoking, thus establishing an association between the act of consuming food and the indulgence in cigarettes. Likewise, you may also be hosting your own gatherings. Therefore, should your attendance be contingent upon your smoking schedule, I kindly request that you make a concerted effort to ensure that your presence coincides with the event, even if only an estimate can be provided.

Therefore, regardless of whether an individual smokes 10 or 20 cigarettes, in the context of moderate smokers, it is imperative that all 10 or 20 cigarettes be appropriately timed. The key lies in the establishment of this schedule.

Smoking electronic cigarette

The prevalence of e-cigarettes on the global platform can be attributed to the dissatisfaction surrounding conventional tobacco consumption. Curiously, an electronic cigarette also poses inherent risks. According to the findings of the Centre for Disease Control and Prevention, e-cigarettes, while not containing tobacco, deliver nicotine to individuals through an aerosol, which also emits potentially harmful chemical substances to both users and those in close proximity.

If you have never engaged in vaping, it is advised to refrain from initiating this behavior at present. The solution you require is not this.

Stages to Stop Smoking

In order to cease tobacco usage, it is imperative to ascertain one's current phase of addiction. When contemplating the enrollment in a new course or training program, individuals possessing a certain level of expertise tend to conscientiously evaluate their proficiency level - be it beginner, intermediate, or advanced - prior to committing.

We will be employing the identical methodology to assist you in achieving permanent cessation of smoking. Let\\\'s get in...

Stage one - the precontemplation phase: In this stage, you have not yet reached a decision regarding cessation, although you have been exposed to information through observation, reading, and education on the hazards of smoking. Your concern for the repercussions is genuine, however, the intention to quit has not yet manifested.

Stage two - the phase of introspection: Having acknowledged and witnessed the inherent hazards of smoking, you are currently in the process of getting ready to quit. However, you require additional motivation and responsibility to ensure your continued progress.

This is the contemplative phase where the inclination to cease smoking intensifies and your motivation amplifies. By engaging in this process, you allow yourself to access knowledge pertaining to smoking and the effective attenuation of its triggers.

Phase three - the preparatory stage: During this phase, you have made the conscious decision to cease smoking, and a tumultuous upheaval is anticipated for anything that serves as a diversion. Upon observation, one can discern that the disadvantages of smoking outweigh the advantages, thus serving as an impetus to embark upon the journey of permanently abstaining from smoking. You are not engaging in mere planning, but rather, you are fully committed to quitting smoking.

Level four - advanced stage: You are consciously and determinedly endeavoring to cease smoking through every available method; you are diligently applying all your resources, determination, and inspiration. You are prepared to handle both internal and external disruptions to your objective of smoking cessation. During this period, it is crucial to receive ample support from friends, family members, and subordinates in order to cease smoking.

Key suggestion: It is essential to request their assistance.

Stage five - maintenance phase: At this juncture, you are transitioning into a state of being a former tobacco consumer. You have acquired methodologies, protocols, and innovative strategies to uphold your commitment and have discovered more efficient techniques to adapt to any situation without experiencing longing or urges. It is conceivable to experience a setback at this juncture; however, through the presence of a committed support team, the odds of such an occurrence are negligible.

The Statement Of The Problem

Nicotine addiction exerts a potent influence, ensnaring numerous individuals and propelling them into a state of dependency fraught with health perils and emotional distress. In the following chapter, we shall explore the issue of nicotine addiction, meticulously analyzing its complex interconnections and the daunting obstacles encountered by individuals aspiring to liberate themselves.

A. Comprehensive Investigation into the Complexities of Nicotine Dependency

Nicotine, an intensely habit-forming compound found in tobacco products and various alternative manifestations, exerts a profound influence on both the human brain and physiology. Upon entering the bloodstream, nicotine swiftly navigates towards the brain where it proceeds to attach itself to designated receptors, thereby activating the release of dopamine, a neurotransmitter that is closely linked to feelings of pleasure and reward. This procedure engenders a euphoric state, further solidifying the inclination to persist in nicotine consumption.

Over a period of time, the brain acclimates to the presence of nicotine, resulting in a state of tolerance and necessitating higher doses for desired outcomes to be achieved. This detrimental pattern exacerbates the addiction, rendering it progressively more arduous to overcome. The physical addiction to nicotine is further augmented by the psychological elements, as the act of smoking becomes entwined with everyday practices, emotional states, and social engagements.

Nicotine addiction is not solely contingent upon an individual's strength of resolve or ability to exercise self-restraint. It entails a intricate interplay among biological, psychological, and social components. It is of paramount importance to comprehend that addiction should not be perceived as a personal deficiency or an indication of frailty; rather, it is a physiological reaction to the potent impact of nicotine on the brain.

To achieve smoking cessation and conquer nicotine dependency, it is imperative to address both the physiological and psychological components. Effectively addressing the psychological triggers and emotional associations associated with smoking is essential for successfully managing the physical cravings. Hence, conventional cessation approaches that narrowly concentrate on sheer determination or substitutes frequently prove inadequate. In order to liberate oneself from the chains of nicotine addiction, it is imperative to adopt a holistic approach that addresses the underlying factors and offers effective strategies to surmount the obstacles encountered at all levels.

B. A Comprehensive Analysis of frequently employed cessation strategies and their inherent limitations

In the pursuit of overcoming nicotine addiction, numerous individuals have undertaken a myriad of cessation methods. There is a wide range of options to choose from, including personal determination, nicotine alternatives, and alternative therapeutic approaches. Nevertheless, these strategies frequently fall short in addressing the inherent psychological and physiological factors that contribute to addiction.

Relying solely on one's strength of mind, a widely employed approach, places a significant burden on the individual, necessitating continuous self-restraint in face of desires and enticements. It shifts the responsibility onto self-regulation, a faculty that can readily falter in light of the formidable hold of addiction. Although individuals may have the utmost intentions, sheer willpower frequently proves inadequate in maintaining long-term abstinence from smoking.

Nicotine replacement therapies such as gums, patches, or e-cigarettes provide a viable substitute for nicotine, facilitating the gradual reduction of dependence. Although they may provide temporary relief from physical cravings, they fail to address the psychological components of addiction. The fundamental patterns of behavior and the connections typically associated with smoking persist unaltered, thereby posing considerable difficulty in completely relinquishing the habit.

Additional treatment modalities, such as the application of acupuncture or hypnotherapy, have also been investigated as plausible interventions for smoking cessation purposes. While certain individuals may perceive these techniques as beneficial, their efficacy may differ among individuals. The efficacy of these methods frequently relies on individual convictions and receptiveness to the particular therapy, rendering them less widely applicable.

7

Money wasted on cigarettes

S

Smoking is a practice that entails considerable fiscal implications for individuals and society at large. The expenditure on cigarettes and associated costs can accrue rapidly for those who smoke, depleting their earnings and potentially compromising their financial solvency and wellbeing. The burden of smoking-associated health issues and reduced productivity poses a considerable strain on societal resources and presents a formidable obstacle for public healthcare systems.

Commencing with the individual level, the financial burden associated with smoking can be overwhelmingly high. In numerous countries, the price of a pack of cigarettes can exceed several dollars, exhibiting regional and brand-related price fluctuations. Throughout a span of twelve months, the expenditure associated with smoking has the potential to accumulate to a significant sum, reaching several thousand dollars. This financial burden restricts a smoker's capacity to engage in future-oriented savings or pursue alternative financial ventures.

Furthermore, apart from the financial implications of purchasing cigarettes, smoking can also incur supplementary expenditures, including augmented healthcare expenses. Individuals who engage in smoking have an increased propensity to encounter a multitude of health complications, such as the occurrence of cardiovascular ailments, cerebrovascular incidents, and malignancies predominantly affecting the lungs. These conditions may necessitate substantial expenditures related to medical interventions and prolonged stays in medical facilities. Additionally, individuals who engage in smoking behavior often exhibit increased instances of absenteeism and diminished productivity. As a consequence, they may experience a decline in earnings and a subsequent decrease in overall income.

The socioeconomic impact of smoking is equally substantial on a societal scale. The financial implications of smoking-related illnesses and diseases on the healthcare sector have a significant impact, imposing a substantial strain on public health systems by depleting resources and elevating healthcare expenses across society. Furthermore, the adverse consequence of reduced productivity resulting from smoking can significantly affect the economy, as individuals are unable to make their maximum contributions to the workforce.

The financial implications of smoking extend beyond the immediate costs involved in maintaining the habit. The repercussions of secondhand smoke on individuals who do not actively smoke, encompassing amplified health hazards and diminished quality of life, can likewise incur considerable expenses upon society. In addition to the financial strain caused by smoking, the environmental consequences such as litter and pollution further contribute to the overall economic burden of smoking.

Ultimately, smoking entails substantial financial repercussions for both individuals and society, to summarize. The cumulative expenses stemming from cigarette expenditure, escalated healthcare costs, and diminished workplace contribution can swiftly accrue, thereby detracting from a smoker's capacity to save and allocate funds for future investments. On a societal scale, the financial burden posed by health issues and reduced productivity resulting from smoking is substantial, rendering it a considerable public health obstacle. In order to alleviate the economic strain associated with smoking, it is imperative to tackle the underlying factors that contribute to this behavior and to offer smokers the necessary assistance and resources to facilitate cessation. This necessitates a prolonged and synchronized endeavor on the part of public health entities, governmental bodies, and societies, in order to foster a future characterized by diminished smoking rates and alleviated financial burdens associated with this behavior.

2: The Significance of Discovering a Holistic Method

I

In your endeavor to cease tobacco usage, you may have come across a multitude of strategies and methodologies aimed at facilitating your liberation from this dependency. An approach to smoking cessation that has garnered considerable significance and has acquired widespread acclaim is the adoption of a natural methodology. This section aims to delve into the significance of selecting a natural approach and its potential to augment one's progress in their pursuit of tobacco cessation.

Section 1: Holistic Well-being

1.1 Identifying and Resolving the Underlying Causes

A holistic approach is centeredaround dealing with the root causes of smoking rather than simply managing the symptoms of nicotine dependency. It recognizes that smoking encompasses not only a physical dependency but also a psychological and emotional attachment. Gaining insight into and effectively tackling the underlying causes significantly enhances your prospects of achieving sustained success in relinquishing smoking.

1.2 Promoting Physical and Mental Wellness

Cessation of smoking encompasses not only the eradication of detrimental substances, but also the advancement of holistic welfare. A holistic approach underscores the restoration and wellbeing of the body and mind through wholesome behaviors and conscientious lifestyle selections. Through the implementation of naturopathic approaches, one can optimize their physical well-being, fortify their immune system, and establish equilibrium in their psychological and emotional states.

Section 2: Reducing Reliance on Alternatives

2.1 Reduced Dependence on Exogenous Substances

Numerous conventional smoking cessation strategies incorporate the utilization of nicotine replacement therapies or pharmaceutical interventions. While these methodologies may prove advantageous to certain individuals, they frequently involve the exchange of one variant of nicotine for another. On the contrary, a natural approach strives to diminish dependence on external compounds through the utilization of alternative techniques that facilitate the regulation of cravings, alleviate withdrawal symptoms, and foster the cultivation of more salutary coping strategies.

2.2 Sustainable Liberation from Addiction in the Long Run

An inherent methodology for cessation of smoking supports autonomy and personal empowerment. Through acquiring the ability to conquer cravings without reliance on nicotine replacement therapies or medications, you cultivate valuable tactics that can be utilized to confront various obstacles in life. This strategy promotes the cultivation of enduring, sustainable independence from addiction, guaranteeing that you are not reliant on external substances to uphold your smoke-free existence.

Section 3: Improving Holistic Well-being

3.1 Supporting Physical Well-being

Cessation of smoking through natural means facilitates the body's inherent ability to restore and rehabilitate itself from the detrimental effects inflicted by smoking. Organic approaches such as utilizing herbal treatments and supplements, have the potential to aid in detoxifying the body, alleviating inflammation, and fortifying the immune system. This emphasis on the overall state of one's physical well-being not only facilitates the process of smoking cessation but also cultivates a more robust and healthful existence.

3.2 Cultivating Emotional and Psychological Well-being

The act of smoking frequently intersects with emotional and cognitive conditions, including but not limited to, stress, anxiety, and ennui. A natural approach acknowledges the significance of fostering emotional and mental well-being throughout the cessation process. The incorporation of mindfulness practices, meditation, and stress-mitigating strategies into a biological framework serves to bolster and promote your emotional welfare.

Conclusion:

Selecting a holistic approach to tobacco cessation presents a multitude of benefits on your path to a life free from smoking. By tackling the underlying factors contributing to smoking, promoting a comprehensive state of well-being, reducing reliance on alternatives, and improving overall health, you lay the foundation for achieving sustained success in smoking cessation. As you progress through the upcoming chapters, I encourage you to adopt the natural methodology, as we will further investigate distinct approaches, remedies, and tactics rooted in nature. These will assist you in your endeavor to quit smoking naturally and lead a healthier, tobacco-free existence.

4: Quitting Smoking

In the following chapter, we will delve into diverse approaches and tactics for ceasing tobacco use, each accompanied by its respective merits and limitations. It is of utmost importance to carefully select the approach that aligns most effectively with your individual requirements and personal inclinations, as doing so will significantly enhance the likelihood of achieving favorable outcomes.

Cold turkey method

The cold turkey approach entails abruptly ceasing the habit of smoking, without the utilization of nicotine replacement therapy (NRT) or medicinal aids. This approach hinges on the cultivation of strong determination and willpower to surmount the discomfort and urges associated with withdrawal.

Advantages:

There are no supplementary charges for nicotine replacement therapy or prescribed medications.

Quicker detoxification from nicotine.

Drawbacks:

Increased likelihood of encountering severe withdrawal symptoms and cravings.

This product may not be conducive to individuals with a significant reliance on nicotine or those who have encountered challenges in quitting tobacco use previously.

Pharmaceutical intervention for nicotine addiction

Nicotine Replacement Therapy (NRT) offers minimal nicotine dosage without the inclusion of the detrimental substances commonly present in tobacco cigarettes. The objective of nicotine replacement therapy (NRT) is to mitigate the manifestations of withdrawal and reduce cravings, thereby facilitating the process of smoking cessation. Nicotine Replacement Therapy (NRT) comes in a range of formulations, encompassing patches, gum, lozenges, inhalers, and nasal sprays.

Advantages:

Alleviates withdrawal symptoms and diminishes cravings.

Offered in various formats to cater to individual preferences.

Most nicotine replacement therapy (NRT) products are readily accessible without a prescription.

Drawbacks:

May be contraindicated for individuals afflicted with specific medical conditions, such as cardiovascular ailments or hypertension.

Excessive or long-term usage could result in the development of nicotine addiction.

Certain individuals may encounter adverse reactions, including dermal discomfort or gastrointestinal disturbances.

Pharmaceutical interventions for smoking cessation

There exist prescription pharmaceuticals that can assist individuals in their efforts to cease smoking, including bupropion (commonly marketed as Zyban) and varenicline (also known as Chantix). These medications operate by selectively targeting the nicotine receptors in the brain, thereby diminishing cravings and mitigating withdrawal symptoms.

Advantages:

Proficient in minimizing withdrawal symptoms and curbing cravings.

Can be utilized in conjunction with nicotine replacement therapy (NRT) to enhance assistance.

Drawbacks:

Necessitates a written order from a qualified medical practitioner.

May result in adverse reactions, including symptoms such as nausea, disruptions in sleep patterns, or fluctuations in mood.

Inappropriate for individuals with specific medical conditions or those who are currently utilizing particular medications.

Behavioral therapy

Behavioral therapy entails collaborating with a qualified practitioner to pinpoint catalysts, cultivate adaptive mechanisms, and acquire proficiencies to effectively combat the inclination to engage in smoking. This form of therapy can be administered on an individual basis or within a communal environment.

Advantages:

Explores the psychological components of nicotine dependence.

Assists in the formulation of enduring strategies for the management of triggers and cravings.

Can be customized to meet individual requirements and preferences.

Drawbacks:

May necessitate a considerable investment of time.

In certain regions, there may be constraints on the availability of qualified professionals.

Alternative methods

Certain individuals may choose to explore alternative modalities in order to cease smoking, including hypnotherapy, acupuncture, or the utilization of natural remedies. Although the scientific evidence supporting these methods may be scarce, certain individuals find them advantageous during their cessation efforts.

Advantages:

Has the potential to offer supplementary assistance to individuals facing challenges with conventional approaches.

Can be employed in tandem with other cessation strategies.

Drawbacks:

There exists a dearth of robust scientific evidence substantiating the efficacy of alternative methodologies.

Could potentially incur significant expenses and may not be eligible for insurance coverage.

To summarize, it can be stated that there is no universally applicable remedy for ceasing the habit of smoking. It is of paramount importance to select the approach that is most congruent with your specific requirements, inclinations, and prevailing conditions. You might discover that employing a blend of strategies yields optimal results for your situation as well. Please keep in mind that ceasing the habit of smoking is a gradual journey, and it is of utmost importance to exhibit patience and perseverance. By employing unwavering resolve, receiving ample assistance, and implementing a suitable methodology, you can triumphantly break free from the grip of smoking, leading to a more salubrious existence devoid of tobacco.

Adverse Health Effects Caused by Tobacco Consumption

Notwithstanding the caution given by God, Adam and Eve ventured to partake of the prohibited fruit. Contemporary society has exerted considerable endeavors to educate individuals regarding the detrimental consequences associated with tobacco consumption. However, there are still individuals who continue to engage in smoking, and there are even those who actively adopt the sentimental allure conveyed through the depiction of discolored lungs in medical facilities or the depiction of a skull adorned with the Red Cross emblem. The custom therefore endures.

Let us analyze the contents enclosed within the pristine packaging of a cigarette.

The principal constituent of tobacco is nicotine, which exerts an influence on the brain. It encompasses over 4000 chemical compounds and 43 carcinogens, a few of which possess toxicity potent enough to elicit deleterious impacts on an individual's physiology. The aforementioned list encompasses an additional 400 distinct toxins, commonly found in both rodenticides and wood varnishes regularly employed.

Hence, it is imperative to take into account the collective consequences.

● Lung cancer, the highly feared illness of our era, predominantly arises due to the consumption of tobacco through the act of smoking. Based on extensive research and empirical evidence, it has been established that smoking is responsible for approximately 90% of the reported cases of lung cancer. Given its impact on the central nervous system, smoking possesses the capacity to induce cancer in numerous bodily organs, including but not limited to the oral cavity, lips, pancreas, kidney, stomach, urinary bladder, larynx, nasal passage, throat, and esophagus.

● Extensive research has established a causal relationship between smoking and the development of leukemia.

● Smoking has a detrimental effect on the quality of coughing and sneezing.

● Research has demonstrated a direct link between smoking and the development of chronic bronchitis and emphysema. ● Smoking exacerbates respiratory distress and worsens the symptoms of asthma. Children who are exposed

Individuals exposed to secondhand smoke have a significantly heightened likelihood of developing pneumonia.

● Pregnant mothers who engage in cigarette smoking are exposed to an increased likelihood of experiencing a miscarriage and

potentially resulting in the delivery of premature infants. In accordance with research findings, neonates born to

Mothers who engage in smoking during pregnancy experienced a reduction in birth weights of their offspring.
- The act of smoking has been demonstrated to exert an influence on human reproductive capabilities.
- Smoking has an impact on an individual's visual perception.
- Tobacco usage has been found to be a significant contributory factor to the development of cardiovascular disorders such as coronary heart disease, encompassing myocardial infarctions and cerebrovascular accidents.
- As per a recent investigation conducted by a scholarly research team associated with the University of Michigan,

Prolonged cigarette usage has the potential to impair cognitive abilities and result in a decrease in intelligence quotient (IQ).

(http://health.indiatimes.com/)

● The act of smoking contributes to the formation of peptic ulcers, which can manifest in various parts of the body.
being the most prevalent.

● Smoking can lead to the development of acid reflux and irritation in the throat, while also affecting every aspect of the metabolism cycle. Individuals who have ceased their smoking habit have indicated experiencing a reinvigorated state.
the level of longing experienced in contrast to their previous smoking habits.

● The act of smoking can lead to the development of vein inflammation and peripheral vascular disease in larger blood vessels.
disorders.

● There is a heightened likelihood of the development of breast cancer among women who engage in smoking.

● The act of smoking can lead to the development of tuberculosis.

- Smoking is associated with various skin ailments.
- Individuals who engage in smoking over an extended period of time have the potential to experience medical conditions such as gastroesophageal reflux disease (GERD) and hypertension. pressure, and insomnia.

1. Dedication and Attitude: Commencing the journey to quit smoking necessitates a resolute dedication and a constructive attitude. It is imperative to have faith in your capacity to cease and uphold a resolute mindset throughout the course of action. Acknowledge that the process of quitting smoking is an ongoingendeavor, and setbacks may arise; however, with unwavering determination and fortitude, one can ultimately overcome these obstacles.

2. Identification of Triggers and Establishment of Coping Strategies: Nicotine addiction frequently encompasses ingrained patterns of

behavior and stimuli. Discerning the circumstances, sentiments, or engagements that elicit the inclination to engage in smoking is an essential measure. Once identified, cultivate alternate strategies for managing stress rather than relying on smoking. Participate in endeavors that foster relaxation, such as engaging in physical exercise, practicing deep breathing techniques, or pursuing fulfilling hobbies.

3. Social Support: Cultivating a robust network of assistance is of utmost significance in the cessation journey. Notify your acquaintances, relatives, and colleagues of your intention to cease smoking and politely seek their comprehension and support. Contemplate the possibility of enrolling in support groups or pursuing counseling as a means of establishing connections with individuals who harbor comparable aspirations. Participating within a community of

individuals who are navigating comparable situations can offer substantial guidance, understanding, and encouragement.

4. Lifestyle Adjustments: Ceasing the habit of smoking frequently necessitates implementing substantial modifications to one's way of life. Discover and adapt behaviors linked to the act of smoking. For instance, if one had the habit of smoking during work breaks, it is advisable to seek alternative pastimes to fill that time, such as going for a stroll or partaking in an alternative social engagement. Furthermore, it is prudent to contemplate embracing a more wholesome way of life in its entirety through the enhancement of dietary habits, participation in consistent physical activity, and the attainment of adequate rest, as these modifications can substantiate your endeavors to cease smoking.

5. Nicotine Replacement Therapy (NRT) serves as an effective method for

alleviating withdrawal symptoms and coping with cravings. Alternatives such as nicotine patches, gum, lozenges, or nasal sprays offer regulated amounts of nicotine, facilitating a gradual decrease in dependency. Seek guidance from a healthcare professional to assess the most appropriate NRT approach for your individual needs.

6. Behavioral Therapy: Behavioral interventions, such as cognitive-behavioral therapy (CBT), can facilitate individuals in conquering the psychological components associated with nicotine addiction. Cognitive-behavioral therapy (CBT) centers its attention on the identification and confrontation of negative cognitive patterns and maladaptive behaviors that are linked to smoking. By means of therapeutic interventions, individuals acquire the skill to reevaluate their thought patterns, cultivate efficacious mechanisms for handling challenges,

and fortify their ability to withstand cravings.

7. Pharmaceutical interventions: In certain instances, healthcare practitioners may proscribe pharmacological treatments explicitly formulated to assist individuals in their efforts to quit smoking. Pharmaceutical agents such as bupropion or varenicline have demonstrated efficacy in mitigating cravings and withdrawal symptoms. Seek guidance from a medical professional to engage in a conversation regarding the potential advantages and disadvantages of these medications.

8. Protection against Recurrence: The recurrence of smoking habits is a prevalent obstacle encountered by individuals striving to cease smoking. It is imperative to perceive relapses as transient impediments instead of shortcomings. Acquire knowledge from instances of relapse, discern the triggers or circumstances that precipitated them, and adapt your approaches accordingly.

Engage in introspection regarding your advancement and recollect the motivations that originally led you to make the decision to discontinue.

9. Stress Management: The experience of stress frequently acts as a catalyst for engaging in smoking behavior, and acquiring efficient stress management strategies can profoundly facilitate your endeavor to quit smoking. Delve into a range of stress mitigating approaches, including the practice of mindfulness meditation, participation in yoga activities, or involvement in pastimes that foster serenity. Implementing effective stress management strategies is essential in mitigating the risk of relapses and fostering holistic wellness.

10. Incentivizing Health: In recognition of your progress in the cessation of smoking, it is advised to indulge in gratifications for each milestone accomplished. Nevertheless, rather than employing cigarettes as a form of reinforcement, consider selecting

healthier substitutes. Indulge in a day of relaxation at a spa, acquire a novel or electronic device, or organize a weekend retreat. Through the use of positive reinforcement tied to cessation milestones, you cement your dedication and inspire yourself to persevere on the journey towards a tobacco-free existence.

Drink water.
Although it is widely recognized that the act of smoking cigarettes enhances the likelihood of developing cancer, heart disease, and lung disease, a significant number of individuals continue to grapple with the challenge of overcoming their addiction to nicotine, despite the well-established health risks associated with this habit. To achieve a successful cessation of smoking, it is imperative to choose the appropriate approach, with one of the most efficient strategies being the substitution of alcoholic beverages or carbonated soft

drinks with water. Achieving a permanent cessation of your smoking habit can be accomplished with the assistance of a single straightforward technique.

It is widely recognized that smoking has detrimental effects on one's health. However, a lesser-known repercussion of smoking is its impact on renal function. Due to the crucial role of kidney filtration in eliminating toxins from the bloodstream, smoking will exert substantial strain on the kidneys, compelling them to function at a heightened capacity in order to eliminate tobacco-related toxins. The kidneys are subjected to undue strain, which may result in the development of kidney disease or even progress to kidney failure. However, there is a positive aspect to this situation: there exists a straightforward method to eliminate these supplementary toxins and safeguard the health of your kidneys, which entails the consumption of water.

If you have previously attempted to cease smoking, it is likely that you have encountered the age-old saying 'Increase your water intake to aid in smoking cessation.' However, if you are currently a smoker, you may question the veracity of this suggestion. What are the potential benefits of consuming water as a means to aid smoking cessation, given that nicotine ingestion from smoking can elicit pleasurable sensations and mitigate the intensity of one's cravings? Indeed, it is widely acknowledged that smoking entails the intake of nicotine, a substance that induces pleasurable sensations and serves to alleviate heightened cravings. Let us examine the rationale behind considering water consumption as the pivotal element in effectively ceasing smoking, along with elucidating strategies to readily integrate this practice into your everyday schedule.

Ceasing the habit of smoking cigarettes can present a formidable challenge, particularly when grappling with the accompanying issues associated with this addiction. Nevertheless, consuming water presents considerably less difficulty, and it facilitates the abandonment of the smoking habit without the undesirable repercussions associated with alternative cessation aids such as nicotine patches or gum. Please proceed with reading to learn the significance of consuming water in your endeavor to permanently quit smoking cigarettes.

Many individuals hold the belief that cessation of smoking solely entails relinquishing nicotine; however, for those truly committed to breaking the addiction, ensuring a sufficient daily water intake is equally crucial. It may be self-evident, yet numerous individuals who engage in smoking fail to adequately hydrate themselves during the challenging experience of contending with the barrage of cravings induced by the symptoms of nicotine withdrawal. This situation can give rise to sentiments of despair along with substantial increase in body weight, both of which can present marked obstacles in the initial cessation of smoking. Whilst endeavoring to overcome the addiction to tobacco, it is imperative to recognize the importance of consuming an ample amount of water, supported by four compelling justifications.

Cessation of smoking is a challenging endeavor, particularly in circumstances where one is burdened with high levels of stress and numerous obligations, compounding the difficulty of overcoming the smoking habit. Consuming water consistently, adhering to the recommended intake of at least eight 8-ounce glasses per day, serves as a means of demonstrating dedication to the cessation of smoking. This is attributable to the fact that adequate hydration aids in the prevention of weight gain, alleviation of nicotine cravings, and maintenance of a healthy and glowing complexion.

Preserve the health of your respiratory system and eliminate the need to expend any financial resources on cigarettes indefinitely.

Post-Quit:
- Exercise patience: Rest assured that any heightened sleepiness or moodiness you may be experiencing is temporary and will subside.

- Remain physically active: Consider engaging in activities such as hiking or biking, which not only help to occupy your time but also enhance your overall well-being.

- Sustain a favorable outlook: Concentrate on the advantages of abstaining from smoking, such as enhanced well-being and serving as a positive role model for others.

- Ingest regular meals: Occasionally, the sensation of hunger may be mistakenly interpreted as a craving to smoke. Therefore, it is vital to partake in consistent meal consumption.

- Establish a fund: Set aside the funds you would have otherwise allocated to purchasing cigarettes within a designated savings account and observe the accumulated savings over a period of time.

- Solicit assistance: Inform others of your decision to cease smoking and solicit support from cherished ones and acquaintances.

Conclusion

Quitting smoking is a difficult process, but it is well worth the effort considering the many positive effects it has on one's health. You will be able to improve not only your overall health and well-being but also your chances of being successful if you put the advice and suggestions contained in this to use. Don't give up if you have a relapse and go back to smoking; many people who have successfully kicked the habit smoked for many years before they were eventually able to do so. Continue your efforts, and don't waver in your dedication to achieving your objective of quitting smoking.

The Closing Chapter: The Many Advantages of Giving Up Smoking

Congratulations for deciding to finally kick the habit of smoking. If you stop smoking, you will notice improvements almost immediately, including an improvement in your ability to taste and smell your food, an improvement in the scent of your breath, and a disappearance of your cough. These advantages are shared by healthy people and those who already have a disease or condition that is brought on by smoking, as well as by men and women of any age, including older people, and by those who are already suffering from a smoking-related illness.

Putting an end to one's smoking habit is associated with a considerable reduction in the chance of a variety of health issues, such as lung cancer, as well as many other types of cancer, cardiovascular disease, stroke, lung disorders, and other respiratory illnesses. Ex-smokers had fewer days of illness, fewer health complaints, and a lower risk of developing bronchitis and pneumonia, according to studies, which shows that they are in better health overall than current smokers.

Quitting smoking not only has a positive impact on your health, but it can also help you save money. Quitting smoking will allow you to have more money in your pocket to spend on other activities, as the expense of cigarettes and the treatment of ailments caused by smoking can add up over time.

Talk to your physician if you feel as though you require more assistance in order to break your addiction to cigarettes. In order to assist you in quitting smoking, they might recommend nicotine gum or a nicotine patch.

In conclusion, if you care about your health and well-being, quitting smoking is one of the best decisions you can make for yourself. Although it is not simple, the rewards are well worth the effort.

Always keep in mind to be patient with yourself, and try not to get down on yourself if you make a mistake. Continue your efforts, and don't waver in your dedication to achieving your objective of quitting smoking. Don't forget: you can get through this!

Comprehensive Manual For Permanent Cessation Of Tobacco Usage

The purpose of this guide is to provide assistance to individuals who engage in regular tobacco smoking, with the aim of facilitating cessation. No matter if you consume cigarettes sporadically or extensively on a daily basis, this comprehensive manual will provide assistance if you meticulously adhere to its instructions and exhibit unwavering commitment. Peruse the text at a leisurely pace on multiple occasions, after which commence the necessary arrangements in accordance.

It is possible that you may harbor the belief that you "are unprepared to discontinue smoking," or that you "must possess the desire to cease this habit in order to effectively overcome it" or even that you "derive pleasure from smoking as it aids in relaxation, making it inconceivable to envision a life without it." However, I can assure you that these assertions are merely mental justifications employed as a means of postponing or impeding your decision to quit smoking and progress towards a life characterized by liberty, improved well-being, and heightened contentment.

All individuals who smoke can be seen as chemically dependent on substances. Nicotine serves as the principal substance in question, whereas the cigarette functions solely as a nicotine administration medium, facilitating the introduction of nicotine into your system and subsequently engendering addiction. Through extensive periods of research and development undertaken by tobacco corporations, this mechanism has undergone a progressive transformation over an extensive span of time. Its purpose lies in nailing down a flawless approach to ensnare individuals into the addiction of their substance, while concurrently enabling these companies to accumulate boundless financial resources, all at the cost of compromising your well-being and vitality.

Unless you cease your actions entirely, a facet of your being will persistently resist cessation.

Kindly ensure a thorough understanding of this matter without allowing it to discourage you. You possess immense strength of character, there is no need to feel apprehensive about relinquishing this substance. It is entirely possible for you to experience tranquility without relying on a cigarette, and undoubtedly, you have the capability to lead a fulfilling life without them. Therefore, let us commence.

One

Three essential factors will serve as the foundation for your permanent transition to a smoke-free lifestyle. These factors include:

PREPARATION, PREPARATION, PREPARATION!

Thorough preparation is pivotal. It is remarkable how some individuals can awaken one day, decide to quit smoking, and effortlessly abstain from it, seamlessly resuming their lives with lasting contentment. These individuals represent the rare circumstances, and if the cessation of smoking was as effortless for every individual, smoking would be completely eradicated. For the majority of smokers, ceasing the act of smoking necessitates a slightly higher level of commitment.

Please bear in mind that if you happen to be a regular smoker, your body and mind have, over an extended period, developed a profound dependence on a highly potent substance. To disengage from reliance on the aforementioned substance and to enable yourself to overcome the belief of dependency, it is imperative to exert diligent endeavor, which necessitates a considerable amount of time and, naturally, proper preparation.

To attain a state of mindfulness and maintain a sense of agency

Mindfulness is an essential component of stability, providing individuals with the ability to exert agency over their circumstances at any given juncture. Exercising mindfulness serves as a mechanism to bring your attention to each and every event and behavior you are about to engage in.

Smoking may occur as a reflexive response, particularly in cases of addiction. Certain individuals have observed a correlation wherein the more they succumb to the urge to smoke, the diminished ability they possess to exercise control over unrelated actions, such as unnecessary purchases, impulsive speech, and even more consequential behaviors like disregarding safety while crossing busy roads. When inquired, they assert that their motivation stems from the emotional gratification it provides, evoking feelings of exhilaration and sending shivers down their spine.

There are few individuals who can genuinely link their impulsive actions with smoking; however, those who recognize the extent of its influence are keen to relinquish such conduct. The sole means to surpass that is by cultivating an awakened state of mindfulness.

The aspiration for mindfulness and a sense of self-command compels individuals to seek cessation from smoking. Mindfulness prevents you from engaging in any undesirable behaviors beforehand. It has the potential to serve as your underlying motivation, and let me assure you, it is a highly formidable motivation.

Your physiological functions are deteriorating.

Extensive research has demonstrated that smoking is causally linked to the harmful deterioration of nerve and blood cells, resulting in a variety of physiological dysfunctions within the human body.

Certain individuals opt to cease smoking once they become aware that the intake of nicotine hinders their bodies' ability to heal effectively as a result of insufficient blood circulation. At times, the situation surpasses mere inadequate recovery and manifests as an impediment to essential functions such as respiration, ambulation, or the execution of routine activities.

The stigma is immensely pervasive.

While it may not be a paramount factor, a significant number of individuals opt to cease smoking due to their inability to cope with the social stigma associated with the habit. In contemporary times, there exists a widespread awareness and dissemination of knowledge regarding the hazards associated with the consumption of cigarettes and marijuana.

In contrast to your possible assumptions, certain individuals who smoke, including yourself, do not derive satisfaction from being subjected to censure or evaluation. While some individuals may interpret this as an appeal to exercise greater discretion in their smoking habits, a small fraction of individuals perceive it as an indication to permanently cease smoking. Frequently, there exist additional contributing factors aside from the societal disapproval, such as desiring to partake in extended periods of social engagement with cherished individuals without relying on a smoking apparatus.

Health consciousness

Are you aware of the consequences that occur whenever you sketch on a cylindrical object and expel vaporous emissions? Your cardiac rhythm and arterial pressure decrease, thereby potentially impairing the cardiovascular system over an extended duration. Furthermore, based on empirical evidence, it can be inferred that a significant proportion of individuals diagnosed with lung cancer, approximately 90%, associate the onset of their illness with the habit of smoking tobacco products.

Certain individuals who have formerly engaged in smoking behaviors, almost as if influenced by a supernatural force, experience a sudden realization regarding the detrimental effects their habits have on their well-being, prompting them to make the conscientious decision to cease smoking. This realization may be prompted by a fresh and compelling purpose in life, such as the arrival of a new child or the acquisition of a new job. Additionally, as my friend mentioned previously, it could also stem from a desire to establish proximity to one's family.

Consider the following: Is it possible for an individual contending with respiratory ailments to derive pleasure from engaging in outdoor activities such as hiking, running, or partaking in leisurely pursuits with dear ones?

Listening to individuals' narratives of triumph in their battle against tobacco addiction.

One of the primary factors contributing to smoking is the pursuit of positive emotional states, wouldn't you agree? However, there is an additional sensation that stems from liberating oneself from the clutches of nicotine.

- the substance present in tobacco that engenders addiction to smoking (further details on this matter will be provided shortly). - the addictive component found in tobacco that contributes to smoking addiction (additional information will be presented shortly). That sensation is commonly referred to as relief, but it is occasionally associated with a sense of liberation. Certain individuals choose to cease their smoking habits upon being exposed to testimonies of former smokers who have undergone transformative experiences akin to their own. When one encounters narratives pertaining to the reduction of facial wrinkles, darkened lips, discolored teeth, or thin lips, and the subsequent enhancement of one's self-perception and confidence, curiosity is aroused and one begins to envision a comparable outcome in their own life. The aspiration for an improved existence and the chance to partake in a captivating future propel

Individuals who engage in smoking behaviors are encouraged to contemplate and ultimately make the choice to cease their tobacco consumption.

It is permissible if you fall into this category.

The Pathway Towards Rehabilitation

When addressing the recovery process for individuals struggling with a smoking addiction, it is essential to recognize the four primary elements that contribute to the restoration of their well-being.

Upon cessation of nicotine consumption, the nicotine will be eliminated from the body within a period of 72 hours.

1. Physical Withdrawal - Nicotine attains its maximum effect within a span of two hours and requires replenishment at the same frequency. Once nicotine is discontinued, the residual nicotine present in the bloodstream undergoes a series of metabolic transformations before being eliminated completely from the body within a duration of less than three days. The period during which nicotine requires to readjust after cessation is typically within a span of two to three weeks, during which the brain will acclimate and commence functioning independently, without the reliance on nicotine in any form. The sensory responses of the brain at a neurochemical level. However, the key factor lies in persevering with your recovery.

2. Subliminal Stimulus Eradication - This occurs when a smoker has conditioned their cognition and subconscious faculties to anticipate the consumption of nicotine during precise instances,

settings, endeavors, associates, or emotional states. Ceasing the consumption of nicotine in the initial days to weeks can be an arduous task. Once an individual perseveres and exercises self-control for a duration of approximately one month, the inclination will diminish significantly and the physiological system will commence the process of reestablishing equilibrium.

3. Self-examination reveals that the reliance on these substances poses a significant challenge, leading to detrimental repercussions in the lives of smokers and causing disruption within their households. It is recommended to lead a lifestyle that is self-reliant and free from any reliance on chemical substances. Anticipate engaging with a minimum of six distinct emotional stages: denial, anger, bargaining, depression, acceptance, and complacency.

4. Mindful existence - adopting mindful existence represents the final crucial stage in the process of smoking cessation. It is indeed related to the prior memory that has been previously stored within the cerebral regions. It is necessary for individuals to exercise self-discipline and lead a mindful existence.

Initially, the journey may pose challenges; however, the urge experienced by smokers to indulge in another cigarette will progressively diminish on a daily basis. The cravings experienced initially may be quite intense as the individual has recently quit smoking, causing the brain to remain wired to the habitual act of smoking. On a daily basis, by abstaining from smoking, there will be a gradual rewiring of their neurological pathways, enabling them to effortlessly navigate through entire days without succumbing to the cravings for nicotine. In due course, you will cultivate the practice of leading a nicotine-free existence sans any contemplation or desire thereof. Withdrawal Symptoms - as the name suggests, they are considered impartial and cannot be classified as positive or negative. Ceasing abruptly without knowledge and understanding can instill fear and apprehension. All pharmaceuticals utilized for smoking cessation exhibit a shared characteristic, namely the capacity to modulate the re-sensitization of brain neurons to varying extents. Consequently, internal confusion will arise as your body encounters uncertainty regarding its course of action. This phenomenon is considered within the realms of regularity as the human body tends to readjust gradually to its pre-pharmaceutical product state due to a lack of familiarity with being substance-free. Nevertheless, there is no cause for apprehension since this is an inherent physiological reaction indicating our body's need for assistance in achieving cessation. It tends to persist even among individuals who desire to quit smoking, particularly when they become accustomed to the addiction. There are certain habits that need to be cultivated and important considerations to be taken into account when attempting to quit smoking abruptly, such as the following: Documenting Your Motivations - When individuals who are addicted to nicotine find themselves in the midst of the struggle, they often struggle to vividly remember the many reasons that initially inspired them to start their journey towards quitting.

Three-Day Duration of Natural Juices - Unless precluded by health conditions or dietary restrictions, it is recommended to consume ample amounts of natural acidic fruit juice during the initial three-day period. Cranberry is awesome. Acidic juices contribute to expedited elimination of the alkaloid-induced relaxation during an emergency. It is strongly advised to adopt a progressive approach by gradually reducing smoking habits, such as taking regular hour-long breaks without indulging in smoking, and subsequently rewarding oneself to commemorate the achievement. Systematically amplify this.

It is important to remember that the onset of illness cannot be attributed to the utilization of any specific stimuli, as long as nicotine does not enter the bloodstream. The majority of triggers are managed and executed by a solitary occurrence, during which the subconscious mind fails to acknowledge the expected outcome. We ought to perceive every individual occurrence as a bestowed privilege and a testament to the unfolding of a new phase in life.

2 – Establishing the Target Date for Cessation of Smoking

Once you make the decision to cease your smoking habit, it is imperative that you select a significant date to commence this process. This day holds immense significance as it presents you with a momentous occasion to commence afresh. This date marks your intended cessation of [activity] Ideally, it is preferable for the deadline to be in close proximity to the present date, as selecting a date too remote could risk forgetting the task, while opting for a date too immediate may induce a sense of haste. Typically, it is advised by professionals to wait for a period of one month following your decision day. A period of one month should suffice for you to engage in thorough reflection, strategic planning, and effectively convince yourself of the viability of the proposed course of action. To offer assistance, kindly observe the subsequent procedures to enhance your readiness in the process of terminating your current position:

Please designate a date and mark it on your calendar. Ensure that your calendar remains visible. For an accurate and comprehensive reminder, it is essential to ensure that all of your digital calendars are synchronized to reflect the intended cessation plan.

Formal alternative: "Express your intention to cease participation to your family members and friends." After you have determined the specific date on which you will cease the habit, communicate this information to your family and acquaintances. Inform them that you intend to solicit their moral backing.

Ensure that an adequate quantity of cinnamon sticks, sugar-free gum, hard candy, and carrot sticks is available to resist the temptation and counteract the fixation.

Develop a comprehensive strategy. Consider inquiring, "Have you been provided any alternatives for cessation by the health center or your healthcare provider?" Moreover, which of the recommended methods is most suitable for meeting your specific needs? Which helpline or web-based support network can one avail themselves of when encountering challenges while striving to discontinue the habit? Once you have acquired this information, you may proceed to record the specifics of your proposed course of action.

*) If you desire to pursue a completely natural and utterly wholesome approach to cessation, it is advisable to refrain from experimenting with nicotine replacement therapy. Typically, the utilization of gums and patches has the potential to modify one's body metabolism, thereby potentially causing an imbalance in hormonal levels. This accounts for the occurrence of hot flushes in individuals who turn to these or comparable oral medications. While they may enhance the likelihood of

achieving favorable outcomes, it remains possible to abandon your endeavor even in their absence. Offset this challenge by harnessing your unwavering determination to successfully abandon this habit.

*) If feasible, consider enlisting in a smoking cessation course to avail yourself of additional knowledge pertaining to your endeavours in all-natural cessation, driven by sheer will.

*) Make an effort to repetitively articulate the following phrase: "I do not engage in the act of smoking." I am grateful for your generous offer. By consistently expressing this sentiment, you will gradually develop a genuine belief in the statement.

If you are acquainted with an individual who is also considering quitting, you could engage them as your cessation companion. Please ensure to support one another and offer encouragement during moments of emotional distress. Should you desire to do so, you could consider the option of attending Nicotine Anonymous as a collective endeavor. Ensure that progress is monitored daily by conducting regular check-ins. Ensure that you are well acquainted with your individual smoking triggers. It is imperative that you document the factors that incite and compel you to engage in smoking. Consistently consider instances when one would typically reach for a cigarette and a lighter. Please bear in mind all of your customary practices. Envision those concepts visually, or alternatively, transcribe them comprehensively. After you have successfully resolved all of them, deliberate upon the most optimal alternative to smoking. You may consider consuming coffee as an alternative. Perhaps, rather than indulging in smoking, you may consider taking a leisurely stroll following a substantial meal. Through the identification of triggers, one can effectively reduce the degree of exposure to sources of temptation.

*) The fear of weight gain deters some individuals from even considering cessation. If such a circumstance exists, it would be prudent to endeavor to attend the gym on a consistent basis. Rather than idling, engage in physical pursuits to better occupy your time. Through engaging in increased physical activity, one will discover that the act of smoking becomes significantly less prominent in their thoughts. Moreover, you will experience an enhanced sense of self-esteem.

In addition, authorities have identified the prevailing challenges associated with determining the cessation date. As previously stated, the significance of this date necessitates careful consideration on your part. Presented below are a number of recommendations put forth by these esteemed professionals:

*) Selecting tomorrow as your desired cessation date is not recommended. Please bear in mind that this is a significant undertaking, requiring you to readjust your lifestyle and habits, while abstaining from the use of tobacco products. As a result, it might be necessary to allocate a considerable amount of time in order to adequately enhance your level of preparedness. The preparations extend beyond the realm of the physical, thus it is advised to select a date that allows for ample time and adequate preparation. And without a doubt, selecting tomorrow will not be effective.

Tomorrow holds no significance. Next year is also not a preferable option. According to expert consensus, it is deemed infeasible to establish a date that falls within an exceedingly remote future timeframe. Humans have a tendency to inadvertently overlook even the most significant dates. Therefore, it is important to consider that, despite the ample time granted by the encounter of "next year," you should not underestimate the possibility that your motivation or inclination to quit may have dissipated by that point. Typically, the optimal duration spans between a fortnight and a month.

*) It is advisable to refrain from selecting a date that aligns with a major social gathering involving friends and relatives. That has the potential to compromise the entirety of the plan. Dates of this nature are commonly identified as days possessing inherent obstacles. They typically entail a greater number of difficulties, rendering failure a likely outcome on such occasions. Instances of dates include your anniversary, birthday, and designated holidays. In contemporary times, it becomes increasingly challenging to anticipate whether acquaintances will inadvertently subject you to conventional smoking stimuli. Additionally, you may encounter

challenges when attempting to draw parallels between your experiences during this period and your typical routine. To the best of your ability, kindly select a day that closely mirrors a typical or customary day in your everyday life.

Reasons To Stop Smoking

It is widely acknowledged that the act of smoking cigarettes is detrimental to our health, however, what are the compelling reasons for individuals to cease this habit? What are the actual expenses associated with smoking a few cigarettes on a daily basis?

Let us begin with the evident choice.

It has an impact on your well-being.

The act of tobacco use is the paramount contributor to avoidable fatalities within the United States. The inhalation of second hand smoke and the act of smoking cigarettes contribute to an estimated 400,000 fatalities solely within the borders of the United States.

The act of smoking cigarettes is associated with the development of various forms of cancer, such as those affecting the esophagus, lungs, larynx, mouth, throat, bladder, kidney, cervix, pancreas, and stomach. Additionally, it has the potential to induce myeloid leukemia, cardiovascular ailments, and cerebrovascular incidents. Furthermore, it can result in a range of cardiovascular ailments, including asthma, emphysema, bronchitis, and exacerbations of existing pulmonary conditions.

Smoking likewise has an impact on cognitive function. Based on research conducted at the National Institute of Drug Abuse, it has been found that nicotine addiction can result in enduring chemical alterations in the brain that bear striking resemblance to the changes instigated by addiction to cocaine or heroin.

Fortunately, it is still possible to mitigate the adverse consequences of smoking. Indeed, research indicates that the cessation of smoking by the age of 30 significantly mitigates the progression of smoking-related illnesses by 90 percent. Ceasing cigarette consumption at the age of 50 can also ameliorate the mortality rate associated with smoking by 50 percent.

Upon cessation of smoking, the individual's blood pressure and heart rate will gradually resume their normal levels. The concentration of carbon monoxide also commences a gradual decrease. The cardiac circulation and myocardial function will also undergo enhancement. The taste of the food will gradually become more pleasurable while your olfactory perception begins to enhance. After the lapse of one year upon cessation, the risk of acquiring cardiovascular disease is diminished by fifty percent.

It has an impact on your financial situation.

No surprise here!

Engaging in smoking incurs significant financial costs. Indeed, you would be astonished by the considerable amount of money you expend on cigarettes annually.

Suppose you currently engage in the habit of consuming a pack of cigarettes per day, and it has been your consistent practice for a span of 15 years. The standard retail price for a package of cigarettes is usually $8. If one were to consume a pack of cigarettes per day, they would have expended a total of $29,200 over the course of the past decade. The magnitude of this financial outlay is quite substantial indeed. You had the opportunity to allocate those funds towards more productive endeavors instead of engaging in self-destructive behavior.

Furthermore, it offers additional financial advantages. It facilitates cost savings on healthcare expenditures, as previously stated, as abstaining from smoking will consequently mitigate the likelihood of contracting specific illnesses.

Smoking diminishes one's appeal to potential romantic partners and employers.

Tobacco use exerts adverse effects on the skin and overall aesthetic appearance. Therefore, ceasing tobacco use yields numerous aesthetic advantages. It imparts a more youthful appearance. Additionally, a study conducted in Zurich reveals a significant link between the occurrence of gray hair and smoking habits, owing to the potential harm caused by nicotine and various chemical substances present in cigarettes to the cellular structure of hair follicles. Additionally, the act of smoking has the potential to restrict blood flow within the facial region, thereby increasing the likelihood of developing wrinkles.

An encouraging fact is that the cessation of smoking can effectively reverse the visible effects of aging within a span of two weeks. Upon cessation, your dental enamel will experience enhanced whiteness, while your oral exhalation will become more pleasantly fragrant. Furthermore, your hair and attire will exude a more pleasant fragrance, and your oral hygiene will visibly enhance.

Resigning also provides the opportunity to discover a compatible counterpart. According to a survey carried out in the United States, approximately 48 percent of the participants expressed a lack of inclination towards initiating a romantic relationship with individuals who smoke. Therefore, if your objective is to enhance the likelihood of finding a desirable partner, it would be advisable to cease partaking in tobacco consumption.

Resigning can bolster one's self-confidence and augment one's vitality. It imparts a sense of increased personal agency and autonomy.

It has an impact on the individuals in your social circle.

Exposure to environmental tobacco smoke poses significant health risks. Based on a comprehensive study, it has been established that each year, approximately 7000 fatalities occur due to lung cancer and about 33,000 deaths result from heart disease, all attributed to the inhalation of secondhand smoke. Between the years 1964 and 2014, an estimated 2.5 million individuals succumbed to the effects of secondhand smoke.

Secondhand smoke comprises numerous carcinogenic compounds such as benzene, formaldehyde, vinyl chloride, hydrogen cyanide, and arsenic ammonia. It has the potential to induce cardiovascular incidents, malignancies affecting the larynx, stomach, breast, rectum, bladder, brain, nasal sinuses, and pharynx. The exposure of children to secondhand smoke poses significant health risks. Indeed, it is accountable for approximately three hundred thousand occurrences of respiratory tract infections in children under 18 months. Therefore, if you desire to safeguard your loved ones, particularly your children, from the harmful effects of secondhand smoke, it is advisable that you cease the habit of smoking. If you are unable to cease this behavior for your own sake, I implore you to consider doing so for the sake of those you hold dear.

Strategies for Mitigating the Risk of Tobacco-Associated Disease

Smoking has the potential to result in severe health complications, hence the optimal approach lies in abstaining from initiating smoking altogether. If an individual engages in cigarette smoking, it is important for them to be aware that promptly ceasing this habit will assist in avoiding or potentially reverting undesirable health consequences. If you abstain from smoking cigarettes, you will be able to:

Minimize the duration of hospitalization.

You will experience a reduced likelihood of contracting other illnesses.

You can expect to experience enhancements in your physical well-being and a pronounced increase in your vitality.

Achieve enhanced aesthetics and bolstered physical well-being.

Enhance your olfactory and gustatory capabilities.

Help the budget.

How To Quit Smoking

There are numerous approaches available to individuals who wish to cease smoking. It is imperative for your success to identify a cessation strategy that aligns with your individual disposition. Put simply, you must be both cognitively and emotionally prepared. Cease the act of smoking for your own benefit, rather than solely to protect those in your vicinity from the harmful effects of secondhand smoke.

Alternative Approaches for Smoking Cessation

The abrupt cessation of smoking, commonly known as "quitting cold turkey," is widely recognized as the most prevalent approach. The probability of success upon initial attempt seems low; however, through unwavering dedication and tenacity, one may eventually achieve the desired outcome.

Nevertheless, had they employed an established and proven treatment approach, a significant number of individuals would have been capable of relinquishing the habit of smoking well in advance. Various methods of smoking cessation, including but not limited to hypnosis, acupuncture, herbal remedies, and alternative approaches, are often advocated. Certain individuals have undeniably achieved success in ceasing their smoking habits through the utilization of these approaches, although there lacks sufficient evidence to suggest their superiority over the sheer act of making a resolute decision to quit.

Well-established methods can greatly assist individuals who are undergoing physical withdrawal symptoms, which can manifest as a reduced ability to effectively carry out tasks in their professional setting (with many individuals facing challenges in terms of maintaining focus and concentration on their work responsibilities).

The World Health Organization, along with various national cancer organizations, are reputable sources of current information regarding the most recent smoking cessation methods and medications. Presently, there are pharmaceutical products in the development phase aimed at aiding individuals in reducing their tobacco consumption in cases where complete cessation is unattainable. Additionally, there is ongoing research on a vaccination that holds promise in preventing individuals from reverting back to smoking after successfully quitting.

Please find below a list of recommendations to consider when you reach the decision to terminate:

❖ Discard all cigarettes and smoking paraphernalia, including lighters and ashtrays.

Are you considering residing with another individual who also engages in tobacco consumption? Kindly ensure that they maintain a distance from you while smoking, or preferably, persuade them to quit smoking alongside you.

✧ Engage in activities to divert your attention during times of craving. The temporary nature of your cravings implies that redirecting your focus away from them and onto your reasons for quitting might be beneficial.

❖ Engage in a kinetic activity such as sketching or manipulating objects like a pen or a straw. Cease engaging in any activities that evoke associations with smoking. Rather than engaging in a smoke break, opt for a leisurely stroll or immerse yourself in a good book.

❖ Inhale deeply when you experience the temptation to ignite a cigarette. For a duration of 10 seconds, sustain the muscular tension followed by a gradual release. It might require numerous iterations of this approach until the inclination to smoke diminishes. Engaging in the practice of meditation can serve to reduce an individual's levels of stress.

❖It would be advisable to avoid proximity to objects, locations, and individuals that evoke associations with smoking. Participate in a non-smoking collective or frequent establishments that uphold smoke-free policies, such as cinemas, cultural institutions, retail outlets, or public libraries.

Do not attempt to quit smoking by relying on confectionery or other edible alternatives. Weight gain may occur as a potential adverse outcome of these substances. Rather, opt for nourishing alternatives that possess a low calorie content. Please consider sampling chewing gum, sugar-free hard candies, celery sticks, or carrots.

❖ Maintain adequate hydration levels by increasing your intake of non-alcoholic and non-caffeinated beverages while reducing the consumption of alcoholic and caffeinated drinks. They have the potential to incite a propensity for smoking.

Embrace the fact that you are a non-smoker and abstain from smoking with pride.

❖ It is advisable to engage in regular exercise as it yields numerous health benefits and helps alleviate stress levels.

May I inquire whether it is still possible for me to cease smoking if I have been engaged in the habit for a significant duration?

Ceasing the habit of smoking confers health advantages regardless of one's age. The long-term impacts of smoking can be reversed.

Welcome to the definitive guide on overcoming your tobacco addiction.

In the forthcoming publication, you will delve into the thrill of emancipating oneself from the habit of smoking. If you diligently incorporate the knowledge that I am about to impart, you shall witness an array of remarkable advantages throughout your journey:

Save money. Cease allocating financial resources to organizations that lack concern for your well-being, which promote and distribute products with the awareness that they have detrimental effects on your health.

Assume responsibility for your well-being. Gone are the days of receiving disapproving glances from your physician or experiencing trepidation when attending your annual check-up; instead, you can now embody a sense of ease and self-assurance in relation to your physical well-being.

Cease tobacco consumption without the apprehension of experiencing weight gain. You will have the capacity to eliminate and substitute a single unfavorablebehavior without substituting it with another undesirable behavior.

Cease your sentiments of being in bondage. You will cease to experience the sensation of being under the influence or dominance of external forces that dictate your daily choices. Partaking in smoking due to necessity or addiction implies that one relinquishes control to the cigarettes and tobacco.

Liberating oneself from those chains is an immensely empowering experience.

Improve your physical fitness. You will regain the ability to engage in running activities and ascend a set of stairs without experiencing shortness of breath.

Become attractive again. No more yellow teeth. Cease the appearance of age and the scent reminiscent of stale tobacco.

Improve your social status. You will be perceived more favorably by others. Children will cease directing their attention towards you in the presence of their guardians.

Does the prospect of enjoying these benefits intrigue you, prompting a desire to incorporate them into your life? Should that be the circumstance, let us proceed to discuss this book and its potential in aiding you on your endeavor to overcome the smoking habit.

Regarding strategies for breaking the habit of smoking

This book is a constituent of a literary collection known as the "Develop Good Habits" series, created in partnership between the undersigned, Jonathan Green, and Steve "S.J." Scott.

Steve is an individual well-versed in the discipline of habit formation and modification, possessing extensive expertise in guiding and supporting others in their pursuit of habit building and cessation. As he has not encountered this particular type of dependency, he is fortunate to have never grasped a cigarette with his fingers. Steve and I have made the collaborative decision to unite our efforts, utilizing a blend of his habit framework and my own firsthand, pragmatic expertise in overcoming the smoking habit.

Collectively, we aim to facilitate a profound metamorphosis in your existence. We shall exchange personal anecdotes and draw upon our wealth of experience in addressing diverse challenges. By virtue of our ardent dedication to enhancing the well-being of individuals, we will also freely divulge narratives from our personal encounters.

This publication centersaround the concept of efficacy, and acknowledges the demanding nature of your daily schedule, hence the intention is to minimize superfluous content and avoid making unsubstantiated assurances. Alternatively, our primary focus lies in providing you with vital information in the most effective and streamlined manner feasible. The objective at hand is to streamline the procedure and support you in embarking on the trajectory towards the eradication of smoking from your existence.

Moreover, numerous literary works offer an abundance of valuable insights aimed at enhancing various aspects of one's existence, yet few delve into the specifics of effectively integrating these insights into one's daily routines. They prioritize theoretical aspects and the underlying reasons, but overlook practical details such as the method and mechanics of smoking cessation, which are of utmost importance.

It is the incremental actions that occur between major concepts that distinguish individuals who are successful from those who fail to meet their goals.

We shall furnish you with a meticulously outlined framework, outlining each step, to enhance your life and yield enduring outcomes within a limited time frame. Our objective is to assist you in replacing the habit of smoking expeditiously and with minimal discomfort.

A portion of the content featured in this book shall inevitably be restated in subsequent volumes of the series, owing to the inherent requirements of the series structure. Our observations have revealed that nearly all habits adhere to uniform and reproducible stages. Hence, we believe it to be imperative to furnish you with a structured approach that enables you to establish or eradicate any habit.

Well, that's enough talk.

It is now opportune to initiate decisive measures, thus transitioning from discussing the cessation of your smoking addiction to actively undertaking the process.

www.ingramcontent.com/pod-product-compliance
Lightning Source LLC
Chambersburg PA
CBHW052142110526
44591CB00012B/1823